Table of Contents

Introduction · · · · · · · · · · · · · · · · · 4

chapter 1 · · · · · · · · · · · · · · · · · 6
How Robotics Began

chapter 2 · · · · · · · · · · · · · · · · · 14
Working Robots

chapter 3 · · · · · · · · · · · · · · · · · 24
Improving Robots

chapter 4 · · · · · · · · · · · · · · · · · 34
Thinking Robots

Glossary · · · · · · · · · · · · · · · · 44
Source Notes · · · · · · · · · · · · · 45
Selected Bibliography · · · · · · · · 45
Further Reading and Websites · · · · 46
Index · · · · · · · · · · · · · · · · · 47

Introduction

Imagine, said Hollywood, a world where the robots have become as smart as the humans who created them. Imagine a rebellion where the robots turn against humans. When we watch films such as *I, Robot,* or TV programmes like *Dr Who,* we see this nightmare of robots running amok.

A comic book (*above*) and film, *The Day the Earth Stood Still* (*above, right*), present typical 1950s' images of creepy robots. In 2004, a police officer played by Will Smith (*below, right*) was still worrying about robots threatening humans in the film *I, Robot.*

But we've also seen the future in a fictional galaxy far, far away, where the robots were charming and loyal. In the Star Wars series, C3PO has a very human personality, and he is devoted to his human companions. R2D2 is adorable, but he is also brave and smart.

So which is it? Do we love robots or are we afraid of them? Will the robots that scientists are developing and building chauffeur us around, clean up our mess and save our lives? Or will robots somehow become a threat? Will they turn on us?

While films present a robotic future, science is working on a robotic present. Roboticists – scientists who specialize in the creation of robots – have quite an imagination too. They imagine and create robots designed to help humans in everything from office work to space exploration. They imagine ways to make robots likeable and fun to have around. You may find that what goes on in an average robotics lab is better than any Hollywood film!

chapter 1

How Robotics Began

Humans have always dreamed of building an artificial person, a completely selfless machine that looks like us and does our bidding. Ancient legends tell of people making little creatures called homunculi out of clay, sand or dust. The homunculi could be brought to life with magical spells and sacred words.

In the first century BC Greeks created small devices that could move on their own. But the Greeks did it with science, not magic. They used their discoveries of pneumatics and hydraulics – using air and fluids to operate machines. The Greeks called their creations automata, meaning 'self-activating'. The Greek automata were certainly clever devices. But the Greeks considered the automata works of art. The devices were not yet robots.

In the 1400s AD, Italian artist and inventor Leonardo da Vinci pictured a much more advanced machine. His notebooks contain detailed sketches

In some ancient legends, homunculi were created with a mixture of magic and chemistry.

FUN FACT!

A robot is defined as an automatic machine that can be programmed to perform certain tasks or jobs. Many robots have humanoid characteristics, meaning they resemble humans. They may have human-like faces or limbs. Androids are robots built to have human bodies. They move and function as humans.

of a robot knight run by mechanical discs, gears and pulleys. But da Vinci never built his robot knight. Five hundred years later, an engineer from the United States, Mark Rosheim, studied da Vinci's plans at the Institute and Museum of the History of Science in Florence, Italy. From a modern engineer's viewpoint, da Vinci's design made sense. In 2003, Rosheim and a team of engineers built the robot knight for a British television series. Put to the test, the robot knight stood, sat and raised its arms. The test proved that da Vinci was the first person to design what can technically be called a robot.

Fast Thinking

For centuries after da Vinci, people continued to develop methods of mechanization – building machines that ran automatically, with little help from human workers. Inventors worked to create devices, from wristwatches to adding machines to weaving looms, that were efficient, reliable and capable of running on their own. Mathematicians, too, worked on new systems for making complex calculations (maths and logic problems). These developments in technology and maths led to a new field in the 1900s: computer science.

Computer science went beyond mechanization to study how information itself could be automated. Computer scientists studied how

The Scribe

Swiss clockmakers and watchmakers have long been masters of miniaturization. In 1772, the Swiss inventor of the wristwatch, Pierre Jaquet-Droz, combined miniaturization with automation to create a robotic doll called the Scribe. The Scribe mimics the act of writing. Its head and eyes follow the motion of its right

hand as it dips a pen into an inkwell. The Scribe then carefully writes words letter by letter. A disk inside the Scribe's body determines which word the Scribe writes. The disk has 40 interchangeable pegs, and the pegs can be set to reproduce the characters of any language. In other words, the Scribe is programmable, just like a computer — except, of course, that the Scribe was invented almost two centuries before computers.

The Scribe (left) still works and is on exhibition at the Museum of Art and History in Neuchâtel, Switzerland. The exhibit also includes Jaquet-Droz's other mechanical figures: the Musician, the Artist and the Draughtsman.

machines could be designed to make calculations automatically. They then studied how data (information) could be electronically fed into and stored in the computer. With that capability the computer could apply its calculations to any number of problems. Think of it this way: a clock is mechanized. You set the time and then the clock's parts work together to keep track of it. A computer can be programmed to tell you what time it is too. But it can also be programmed to calculate what time it is in China, what time it will be after 1,564 seconds have gone by, or exactly what time the sun will rise and set on 17 December of next year.

Very early computers made their calculations accurately but not very quickly. The computers were also very large. Some took up entire rooms. They were filled with vacuum tubes, electric switches and wires. They used piles of punch cards, spools of paper and reels of magnetic tape. Also, each computer had to be programmed step-by-step.

As computer science developed, it became focused on making computers faster, smaller and easier to use. Researchers worked on miniaturizing

ENIAC was the world's first electronic digital computer, built in the United States in 1946. It needed an entire room to hold all its parts. To program it, an operator had to connect thousands of wires by hand.

computer parts. All the tubes, switches and wires were replaced by tiny transistors and electric circuits stored in a small piece of material called a computer chip. Computer chips greatly increased computer speed and memory (storage room for programs and data). Miniaturization took computers from the research laboratory into offices, banks and factories. Miniaturization also paved the way for computers to be used in robotics. Once computers were small enough to fit inside a robot, a whole new world of possibilities opened up.

Working for a Living

The word *robot* comes from the Czech *robata*, meaning 'forced labour'. The word was first used in 1920 by Czech playwright Karel Capek in *RUR. (Rossum's Universal Robots)*. In Capek's play, the Rossum Company manufactures robots to do human work. Robots have actually been used in industry and manufacturing for decades. In fact, almost everything we eat, wear or use was worked on, at some stage, by a robot.

In 1913, Henry Ford started using assembly lines in his car factory near Detroit, Michigan, USA. On an assembly line, a car moves down a long

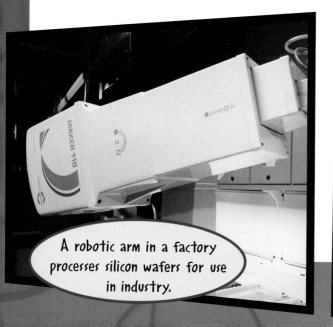

A robotic arm in a factory processes silicon wafers for use in industry.

line of workers who each perform a specific task until the car is complete. Ford loved the efficiency and precision of the assembly line. He would have adored robots, which make up 50 per cent of the modern car industry's labour force. Robots do very well at assembly-line work.

Robotic manipulators weld cars along an automated assembly line.

Most assembly-line robots are computer-operated, multi-jointed arms called manipulators. They do repetitive and dangerous jobs along the assembly line, such as spot welding car bodies, spraying paint on chassis and pouring rubber into tyre moulds. Robot manipulators also work in paper mills, bottling plants, toy companies and factories that make computer parts. These manipulators lift, bolt, fold, stamp, package, weld, remove and replace, hour after hour, for two or three shifts a day.

The manipulators are designed to mimic the motions of the human arm. Some have a ball-and-socket assembly, much like the human elbow. Other manipulators lengthen and pull back by telescoping – that is, their cylindrical sections slide over one another. A third type of robotic arm looks like a huge snake. Robots fitted with four or six of these arms look like metallic aliens.

The arms end in grippers – crude versions of human hands. To be effective, the grippers must match the shape of the item they have to pick up, use or manipulate. Most industrial robots do fine with their grippers, but scientists are developing much more human-like robotic hands. These hands have four fingers and a thumb – capable of providing a grip just like a person's hand.

Flex Those Muscles!

Professor Yoky Matsuoka of Carnegie Mellon University in Pittsburgh, USA, and her team of graduate students are building an anatomically correct testbed (ACT) hand. The ACT hand uses mechanical devices called actuators to work like human muscles and tendons. Matsuoka hopes that the ACT hand can be studied to understand all the complex movements of the human hand. Surgeons may also use the ACT hand as a model for reconstructing human hands damaged by injury or disease.

The ACT hand

The DARPA Challenge

The car industry may have been quick to use the first robots. But it was a group of students, computer scientists and robot builders who met a 2004 challenge to build a robotic car. To encourage research on unmanned vehicles, the US Department of Defense (DOD) set up a race in California's Mojave Desert. The DOD's Defense Advanced Research Projects Agency (DARPA) offered a $1 million prize to the builders of a robotic vehicle that could find its way, unaided, across 229 kilometres (142 miles) of the Mojave's rough terrain. Thousands of spectators lined the course on the morning of 13 March 2004. The robo-vehicles left the starting line packed with computers, sensors and elaborate vision systems. Within a few hours, all the vehicles had either crashed or lost their way. So there was no $1 million winner that day. But competitions and exhibitions like the DARPA Challenge help researchers test new robotics technology.

A robotic car heads to the DARPA starting line.

Roboticists continue to work on creating robots or robot parts that are specially designed for certain types of work. As with the manipulator's 'hand', roboticists often use human or animal models to understand motion, balance and flexibility. The designs roboticists have come up with have taken robots beyond the factory into some pretty amazing places.

chapter 2

Working Robots

There are lots of places we'd like to go but can't. Dangerous places. Distant places. Inaccessible places. We can explore these places by sending in robots. These mechanical daredevils and adventurers have computer brains that don't feel fear or panic. Killer levels of radioactivity? No problem. The black, airless vacuum of space? The crushing pressure of tons of ocean water? Tiny passageways through ancient rock? Bring it on, say these new robots.

On 29 June 2007 a suspicious car was reported parked near a nightclub in London's Haymarket. A police robot was sent in to investigate. The car was found to contain 60 litres of petrol, gas cylinders and nails. The bomb was safely defused and the 1,700 people inside the nightclub were saved from death or injury.

Robots have been used in war zones to find and deactivate land mines (bombs planted in the ground). Robots crept through the choking

Around the world, military and police forces have bomb disposal units. These forces often use explosive ordnance disposal (EOD) robots.

The EOD robots can examine suspicious packages or cars, sparing human officers the danger of being killed or injured in an explosion.

rubble of the World Trade Center towers after the September 2001 terrorist attacks in New York City. Robots have worked at nuclear accident sites in air so contaminated that the robots couldn't be returned to their labs. Robots have been to Mars, and soon they will crawl through human arteries to break up life-threatening blood clots.

You Want Me to Go Where?

In 1994, the National Aeronautics and Space Administration (NASA) teamed up with scientists at Carnegie Mellon University and the Alaska Volcano Observatory to send a robot to explore an active volcano. Scientists explore volcanoes to learn how they work and how to read the warning signs of a volcanic eruption. An eight-legged robo-walker named Dante II climbed down the throat of Alaska's Mount Spurr, 145 km (90 miles) west of Anchorage, USA. Dante's mission was to explore the crater floor and take gas and soil samples. It was something that no human had any intention of doing – not even for the good of science.

Dante's designers knew the descent would be very tricky. The north wall of the volcano has a perilous 300-metre drop and the south wall is steep and covered with rocks. The designers gave Dante a system of servomotors, mechanisms that help Dante's main computer. The servomotors allow Dante to raise and lower each leg individually as the robot climbs over rocky surfaces. Dante's footpads and legs also have sensors to keep it from crashing into rocks or falling into holes.

Even with all this high-tech robo-anatomy, nobody trusted Dante to make its own decisions. Dante was connected to its human team by satellite and the Internet. Its main computer analysed every step before

Dante II makes its way across a snowy path in Alaska.

Why Study Volcanoes?

Volcanic eruptions can kill people and destroy property. The most violent eruptions can destroy entire cities. They can cause huge ocean waves, floods and landslides. Volcanoes can also disrupt weather patterns around the world. Volcanologists (scientists who study volcanoes) can't control eruptions. But through research, volcanologists have learned how to read a volcano's warning signs. Communities near active volcanoes can come up with emergency plans for alerting and evacuating people. In providing research aid to volcanologists, robots help people plan for these natural disasters.

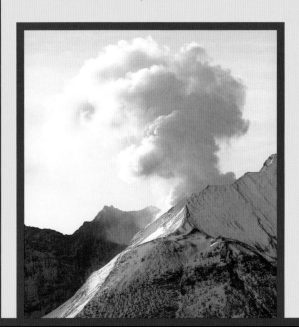

Mount St Helens, an active volcano south of Seattle, Washington, USA, belches out steam in October 2004.

it allowed the robot to go forward. This made Dante one slow robot, but it eventually reached the floor of the crater, safe and sound.

As Dante gathered samples, the robot's stereo cameras relayed a realistic three-dimensional view to the computer screens in front of the scientists at the volcano's rim. Thanks to something called Virtual Environment Vehicle Interface software, the scientists felt as if they were right there in the volcano with Dante.

But a near-perfect robotic adventure ended in a way familiar to anyone who's ever climbed a steep hill. Dante slipped in some loose dirt on the way out of the volcano and could not regain a foothold. Shortly afterwards the science team called in a helicopter to rescue the stranded robot.

The Exploration Rovers collect rock and soil samples and take photographs on Mars.

Unfortunately, no one can take a helicopter to Mars to save the Exploration Rovers if these robots get into trouble. NASA landed twin Rover robots, Spirit and Opportunity, on Mars in 2004 to explore the planet, collect soil and rock samples and take photos. Spirit and Opportunity are all alone on the red planet, millions of kilometres from Earth. Mars is an even more hostile environment than the inside of a volcano. Mars is very cold, averaging −55°C. Its strong winds whip red dust across the rocky surface of the planet.

The Rovers' connection to NASA is tricky too. Communication between the robots and NASA scientists are sent through millions of kilometres of space via computer connections to orbiting spacecraft and antennae on Earth. As the Rovers roll across the Martian landscape, any helpful messages from their human teammates on Earth are delayed by several minutes. So the Rovers are designed to make many of their own decisions. They are given assignments, but it is up to them to work out

Phoning Home

The distance from Mars to Earth varies from 177 to 332 million km (110 to 200 million miles), depending on the planets' orbits. How does NASA maintain communications with the Mars Rovers over that distance? Communications links are provided by NASA's Deep Space Network (DSN). DSN is an international system of very large and powerful radio antennae. The network's communications centres are located in California's Mojave Desert; near Madrid, Spain; and near Canberra, Australia. The communications centres can send commands directly to the Rovers and the Rovers can send data directly back. Often the communications centres relay messages between NASA and the Rovers through other spacecraft orbiting Mars. Relaying messages through Mars orbiters takes less energy for the Rovers.

DSN antennae range in size from about 34 m to about 67 m across. They can send signals to and pick signals up from millions of kilometres away. The Mars Rovers also have four small antennae on board. They can send four different signals to four places at the same time.

how to get them done. The Rovers also have a 'survival instinct' programmed into them, helping them adapt to unexpected situations, such as changes in the terrain.

A Tight Fit

Robots have helped us explore live volcanoes and hostile planets. There are other places to explore that are not dangerous but are simply out of reach to humans. One of those places is inside the Great Pyramid of Giza in Egypt. Modern explorers have long been fascinated by the pyramids – huge structures built thousands of years ago as tombs for Egyptian rulers. Even after hundreds of years of excavation and study by archaeologists, the pyramids still have their secrets.

The Great Pyramid was built around 2500 BC for King Khufu (also known as Cheops). Inside the pyramid, four narrow shafts

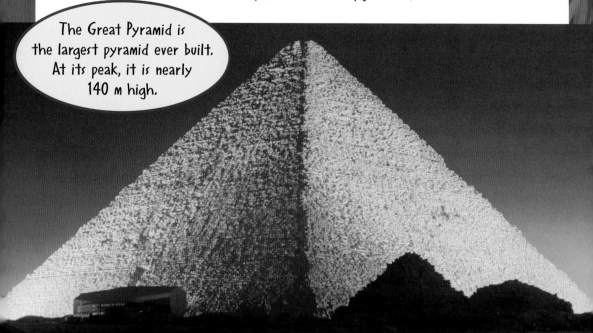

The Great Pyramid is the largest pyramid ever built. At its peak, it is nearly 140 m high.

lead out of two rooms known as the King's and the Queen's Chambers. No other pyramids in the region contain shafts such as these. The shafts are about 23 centimetres high and 22 cm wide. They rise at steep angles from the chamber walls. The shafts in the King's Chamber open to the outer walls of the pyramid. But the shafts in the Queen's Chamber end somewhere inside the pyramid.

When German engineer Rudolf Gantenbrink first visited the pyramid in 1991, he was struck by the mystery of the shafts. It must have been very difficult for the pyramid's builders to include the shafts in their design. So Gantenbrink believed they must have been important, but what was their purpose? And how could anyone explore something so deep and narrow? Gantenbrink thought about it. When he returned to Germany, he began work on a robot small enough to fit in the pyramid's shafts.

After some trial runs, Gantenbrink developed Upuaut-2. Upuaut-2 is made from aircraft aluminium and weighs only 6 kilograms. It is equipped with headlights, a laser guidance system and a miniature video camera. Seven electric motors drive the wheel/track systems, and power is supplied through a cord connected to a generator. Upuaut-2 is also connected to a computer with a video monitor.

Upuaut-2 was the first robotic pyramid explorer. Researchers have since s similar robots into the shafts.

In March 1993, Gantenbrink sent Upuaut-2 into the southern shaft of the Queen's Chamber. Gantenbrink hoped that the videos Upuaut-2 took would solve the mystery of where the shafts ended.

As it turned out, the little robot's journey only deepened the mystery. As Gantenbrink watched outside on the video monitor, Upuaut-2 climbed about 61 m up the shaft. Suddenly, Upuaut-2's camera showed that the robot had been stopped by a stone block in the shaft. The stone was smooth and had copper decorations. It had obviously been placed there on purpose, high up inside the narrow shaft. But by whom, and why? Until another robot with different equipment explores the shaft, the mystery remains.

The Incredible Shrinking Bot

Upuaut-2 was certainly in a tight spot, but a 20-cm shaft is a roomy cruise compared to scientists' plans for the snake-bot. Scientists at the California Institute of Technology are working on the designs for a tiny snake-bot to travel through the human gastrointestinal system (the stomach and intestines). As a doctor looks down a patient's throat for swelling or other signs of illness, the snake-bot would look at a patient's insides. A camera and sensors would help the snake-bot gather medical information for doctors. The snake-bot's information would help doctors diagnose disease and may even help in therapy.

Designed for rescue operations, large snake robots (*below*) can, for example, slither through earthquake rubble to search for survivors. Miniature robots (*above*) from New Mexico's Sandia Laboratory in the USA also explore tight spots.

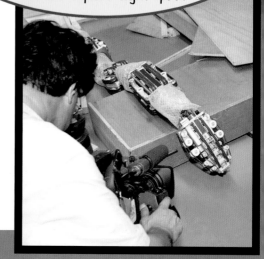

But without question, the tiniest and most daring medical robots are being designed in Sweden. The Swedish micro-bots are smaller than the hypen between *micro* and *bots* in this sentence. The micro-bots are made of silicon coated in gold and then encased in polymer (a plastic compound) that can be made to shrink or swell. This allows the segments of the robot to bend so it can pick things up and move them around.

Sandia researcher Doug Adkins (above) designed the miniature robots to work in swarms, like insects. They communicate with each other and with a central station.

The Swedish micro-bots are designed to be submersible, which means that they can operate in all kinds of fluids. The research team imagines a time in the not-too-distant future when the micro-bots can be injected into the human bloodstream. Doctors hope the micro-bots will be able to clean up the plaque that causes heart attacks and break through the blood clots that cause strokes. The micro-bots could also remove bacteria and maybe even target disease-causing cells.

In the old sci-fi film *Fantastic Voyage,* five scientists and their submarine, the *Blood Vessel,* were shrunk to microscopic size and injected into the bloodstream of a fellow scientist. Their mission was to reach an inoperable blood clot in their friend's brain and save his life. What Hollywood imagined as movie fantasy in 1966 is becoming science fact.

chapter 3

Improving Robots

A sign on the chain-link fence surrounding a factory reads, 'This area patrolled by security guards'. The guards are not what you'd expect though. Instead of uniformed humans, the security force is made up of wheeled robots. The robots use sonar – navigation by sound – to make their way through the empty factory. If one of these robo-guards comes across an intruder, it can alert the police. But it won't be able to wrestle the burglar to the ground, or even chase him, because wheeled robots are very slow.

In a hospital, several robot cafeteria workers deliver meals to the patients. They roll from room to room, neatly avoiding objects and staff members. When necessary, they can even ride in the lift. If something falls off their food cart, however, they can't pick it up. They can't help patients open the cellophane packet containing their plastic utensils. In one case, a service robot, unable to stop itself, fell head over wheels down a stairwell. Wheeled robots can be very clumsy.

These are just two examples of service robots designed to provide daily help to humans. But roboticists know that service robots have a long way to go. The robots will need to be able to negotiate their way around without tripping or becoming confused. They'll need problem-solving skills. Robotic nurses will need legs and arms. They'll have to be able to tell the difference between a patient who is flushed with fever and one who is as pale as a ghost, and decide if one, both or neither needs help. So, in dozens of laboratories in the United States, Canada, Japan, Australia and the UK scientists and engineers are trying to design robots based on the best models of all – those found in nature.

In the early 2000s, some hospitals in China began using robots to perform tasks and carry information.

First Steps

At the University of California, Berkeley, biologist Robert Full is in love with cockroaches. For several years, he has been studying this less-than-adorable creature to find out how it is able to move so fast. After videotaping cockroaches working out on little treadmills, Full discovered that a cockroach doesn't actually run. It bounces, like a pogo stick. This sounds like an unsafe way to travel, but the cockroach solves the problem by using a tripod ('three feet') walk. It has six legs – all insects do – but only three are actually on the ground at any one time. In terms of balance, a tripod is very stable.

Engineers at Case Western Reserve University (CWRU) in Ohio, USA, built a robotic cockroach. The Case robo-roach doesn't have a head, but it does have six legs and a platform body to carry the electronics. It has a tripod walk, and it bounces just like a real live cockroach.

At CWRU, Daniel Kingsley, Roger Quinn and Roy Ritzmann studied real cockroaches (below) to develop their robotic version (above).

Scientists have built several different six-legged robotic creatures, called hexapods. One of the most interesting is Ariel, the robot crab. Ariel was developed by a company called iRobot to scuttle along the beach and on the ocean floor, searching for underwater explosives.

Ariel walks sideways, just like a real crab, and can scramble over uneven ground. Pebbles and ocean surf are not a problem. But the niftiest part of Ariel is the way it can adjust to life's little accidents. If Ariel loses a leg, it can quickly adapt to a five-legged walk. If Ariel is upended, instead of lying helplessly on its back, its legs flip down. The top becomes the bottom and Ariel keeps on going.

You may be thinking that if scientists can build robots with six legs, a two-legged (bipod) robot ought to be easy. But when it comes to legs, the fewer there are the harder it is to keep the robot stable. Unlike the cockroach, which always has three legs on the ground when it is moving, a bipod has only one. So with every step, a two-legged robot must somehow re-establish its balance, or it will fall over.

Harder than It Looks

Nobody teaches us how to walk. Walking is something we more or less work out on our own when we're about a year old. After our leg and back muscles have grown strong enough to support our weight, we pull or push ourselves to a standing position. Then comes the hard part. We want to move forwards — to where mum or the family dog or that shiny toy is. But making it happen takes a little practice. That's because we're bipeds. When we walk, we raise one leg to step forward. All our weight has to be supported by the leg on the ground. But then when we take a second step, we change feet and all our weight has to quickly shift. Learning to shift our weight back and forth is what keeps us from toppling over. After we learn to walk, we branch out to running, jumping, hopping and other motions. Those all involve slightly different skills in muscle control and balance.

Just like us, bipedal robots have to redistribute their weight as they move. But they don't have our learning instincts or sense of balance. To get bipedal robots moving, roboticists study how our muscles and joints work and what techniques we use for balance and control. All this information has to be translated into robot anatomy and computer programs.

Balance is a tough thing to program into robots. But researchers at the Massachusetts Institute of Technology (MIT) Leg Laboratory in the USA, are making remarkable progress. They have built a lot of weird and wacky

robots. Experimenting with these walking, running and hopping robots helps researchers find the most stable and practical leg designs.

Monopod is possibly the strangest robot because it is just one leg and one weight to provide balance. Monopod has joints and a springy foot similar to a humans. It paved the way for Spring Flamingo, the first two-legged lab robot to use its ankles and feet as part of the dynamics of walking. The 3D Biped can perform somersaults, and Uniroo imitates the bounding run of a real kangaroo.

An MIT roboticist takes a test walk with Troody the dinosaur robot. Troody was modelled after a real dinosaur called a *Troodon*. Researchers at MIT's Leg Lab studied *Troodon* skeletons found by archaeologists, to understand how *Troodon* moved.

One of the most exciting robots at the MIT lab is Troody, a two-legged dinosaur robot. Troody is so life-like, it could hitch a ride back to the Cretaceous Era and fit right in.

Together, the MIT Leg Lab robots have strolled, hopped, trotted, bounded and actually run along simple paths, up stairs and over obstacles. One robot hit a running speed of 21 km (13 miles) per hour. Programming a robot to walk like a real animal may be difficult, but it is far from impossible.

ASIMO

In October 2000, Honda Motor Co, Ltd, introduced ASIMO (which stands for Advanced Step in Innovative Mobility) – the world's most advanced bipedal humanoid robot. ASIMO is exactly 1.2 m tall and weighs 52 kilograms. It looks like a spaceman, complete with backpack. (That's where its computer is located.) Honda engineers spent nearly fifteen years of study, research and development to create ASIMO. They would probably say that not a minute has been wasted.

When Honda engineers set out to create a bipedal humanoid robot, they used motion technology to analyse the way human beings walk. A key question was, how do humans transfer weight from one leg to the other when we walk? The engineers worked on ASIMO's legs, which had to be able to make the same complex movements as human legs. Then, as each body part was added to create a humanoid robot, the engineers made adjustments for the new structure and additional weight.

Just like us, ASIMO controls its own walking, and it can stroll along at a leisurely 1.6 km (one mile) an hour. When ASIMO made its debut at the Frankfurt Motor Show in Germany on 9 September 2003, the robot proudly showed off all its skills. It walked backwards, turned corners, climbed steps, shook hands with people and even recognized the faces of a few old friends, addressing them by name. And for the big finish, it even danced around a bit. In 2004 ASIMO was upgraded with a rotating hip that allows it to jog at 3.1 km (1.9 miles) an hour.

ASIMO's amazing accomplishments are the result of the latest developments in electronics, computer science, voice and sound recognition and motion technology. ASIMO can even use networks, such as the Internet, to help it answer people's questions. But what so many visitors to the show found especially remarkable was ASIMO's confident and nearly human stride, a major breakthrough in robotics.

ASIMO greets a student audience during a visit to a school in New York City.

Artsy Robots

The Sony Corporation's QRIO robot took centre stage — literally — in March 2004, when it conducted the Tokyo (Japan) Philharmonic Orchestra. QRIO can perform many tasks. But Sony, a Japanese electronics company, wanted to show off the robot's ability to control its movements. QRIO held a conductor's baton and led the human musicians through Beethoven's Symphony No 5. Japanese car maker Toyota has also proudly produced a musical robot. The Toyota robot can play 'When You Wish Upon a Star' on a trumpet. Toyota says it soon hopes to have an entire robot band ready to belt out tunes.

QRIO (right) and Toyota's trumpet player (below) were both designed to test controlled robotic movement.

Who's Got the Ball?

Robots aren't all work and no play. On 4 May 2003, robots from around the world played football in the International RoboCup Federation's American Open, held at Carnegie Mellon University. Hiroaki Kitano had established RoboCup in 1997 with the hope that it would lead to the development of robotic football players good enough to play against — and beat — human athletes.

That first 1997 tournament was a little chaotic. The robots had a tough time finding the ball, recognizing their teammates and working out which goal they were supposed to aim for. But as engineers improved the robots' vision systems, play improved. By the 2001 games, the 20-cm tall, wheeled robots in the Small League were playing two ten-minute halves on a field the size of a Ping-Pong table. (Their football was an orange golf ball.)

Aibos, robotic dogs, compete in a RoboCup football game.

The Sony Corporation sends its Aibo team to the Open. Most RoboCup players are of the two-legged variety, but the Aibos are little robotic dogs. The Aibos whack the ball by getting down on their elbows. This tail-in-the-air position gives them enough stability to use both front paws. Play is slow and a bit clumsy, but the Aibos are, after all, still amateurs.

Aibos have many motors that allow them to walk, stand, sit and lie down. Aibos are also programmed to bark, find and play with their toys, and take 'naps' when their batteries need recharging. Just like real dogs, they will try to get attention from their owners.

But as wonderful as ASIMO is, it is still, well, robotic. It looks and acts like a robot. However, ASIMO lacks the one thing that humans most respond to in each other: a face. What is going on, we might wonder, behind the black, featureless plate that hides ASIMO's camera eyes? What is it thinking? Nothing, of course. It is not really thinking, only processing. It doesn't really recognize old friends. It simply scans people's features and compares them to data stored in its computer. Its interactions with humans are charming and fun, but we might wish that ASIMO could smile and laugh. We might wish it looked and acted more human. Or do we?

chapter 4

Thinking Robots

Bertram, your robo-butler, rolls into the living room and announces in a flat, mechanical voice, 'Dinner is served.' You're slouched down in a corner of the sofa. 'I'm not hungry, thanks,' you answer. Your parents or friends might ask if you feel alright or if there's anything they can get you. But Bertram has no reaction. He simply rolls back into the kitchen without a word and puts away the uneaten dinner. Bertram has understood your negative reply, but he can't respond to your tone of voice or your body language. Most people, Allison Bruce discovered, really don't like that about robots.

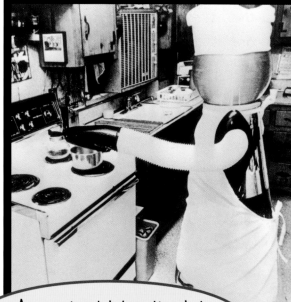

An experimental domestic robot from the 1970s works in the kitchen.

Bruce is a researcher at the Robotics Institute at Carnegie Mellon University. Bruce is part of the institute's Social Robot programme. The programme studies ways to improve interaction between humans and robots. In the experiment, a laptop computer was attached to a robot. The robot stood in a corridor of a college building and asked passing students a question. Sometimes the laptop screen would be blank, but sometimes it showed a computer-generated face with a range of expressions.

Bruce was not really interested in the students' answers to the questions. What she was interested in was the students' willingness to stop and talk to the robot. She found – not surprisingly – that more students responded to the robot when it had a face.

A student pauses to talk with one of the Social Robots at Carnegie Mellon University.

Like Bruce, other roboticists have realized that humans prefer robots they can relate to. Roboticists have developed robots that can express human emotions, such as anger, happiness, embarrassment and sadness.

Fun with Blocks

Lego, the little plastic building bricks, is the stuff of which some robots are made. One of the coolest examples of a Lego-bot is Feelix, built by Dolores Cañamero and Jakob Fredslund at the Lego Lab at Aarhus University in Denmark. Feelix is very good at expressing his feelings. His Lego eyebrows will droop and his mouth will sag when he's 'sad'. If he's 'happy', his mouth turns into a smile and his whole plastic brick face seems to light up.

Cañamero and Fredslund built Feelix from Lego's Mindstorms kit. The kit comes with everything needed to build a robot, including the software and instructions for programming the robot's brain through a personal computer (PC).

Feelix uses its eyebrows and mouth to express feelings.

I Feel, Therefore I Am

Kismet the robot was designed and built by Cynthia Breazeal, a researcher at MIT's Artificial Intelligence Laboratory. The lab is home to a whole assortment of interesting robots. But Kismet is not like the others. This robot can display emotion. Kismet's lips can pout or smile. His eyebrows can arch and his ears can wiggle. But Kismet isn't just a puppet moving his parts around. A combination of clever computer programming and sophisticated engineering has given Kismet the ability to actually respond to a stimulus in an emotionally recognizable way.

If you say words of praise to Kismet, he will smile. Bright colours also earn a smile, as does his own reflection in a mirror. But raise your voice and scold Kismet and his lips will sink into a frown. When Kismet becomes overstimulated by too much noise or movement, he will withdraw, lowering his eyes and taking a kind of robotic 'break'.

Kismet is lovable but not just because of his blue, golf-ball-sized eyes. Kismet interacts with people and shows he has 'understood' them through his facial expressions. His success in relating to people may be reflected in the fact that everyone refers to Kismet as 'he' instead of 'it'.

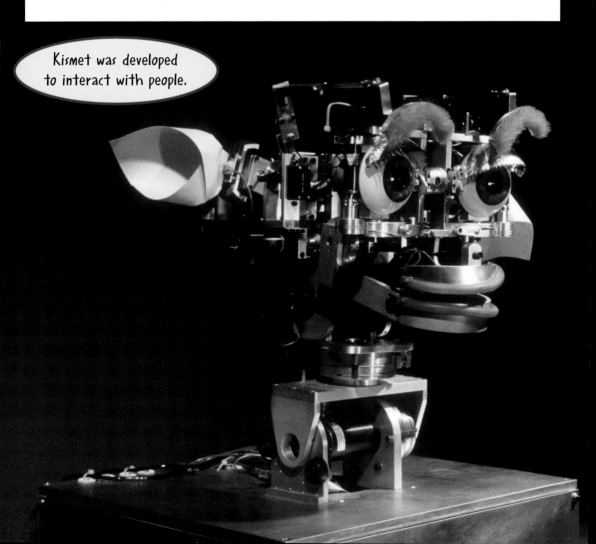

Kismet was developed to interact with people.

Heads Will Roll!

In 2003 a man named Dave Hanson showed up at a science conference in Denver, Colorado, USA, carrying a head. The head was backless and bald and bolted to a wooden platform. It was still rather pretty though, with high cheekbones, blue eyes and smooth rubber polymer skin. Hanson set the head down on a table, plugged it into his laptop computer and tapped a few keys. Everyone stopped to watch what would happen.

Moments later, the head began to move, turning right and left. It smiled, sneered and frowned. Hanson, a roboticist at the University of Texas in Dallas, USA, called the head K-bot. To mimic the major muscles in a human face, K-bot has 24 servomotors under its specially developed rubber polymer skin. The digital cameras in its eyes watch the people who are curiously studying it, and software helps it to imitate what it sees.

David Hanson (*below, right and centre*) designed K-bot to express human emotions.

Hanson has built several robotic heads, but he isn't the only one. In Tokyo, Japan, Hiroshi Kobayashi's face robots, as he calls them, are also eerily life-like. So is the head sitting in Fumio Hara's robotics lab at the Science University of Tokyo. Hara's robotic head can scan the face of the person standing in front of it and compare the face to those in its memory bank. Once the robot identifies which of six emotions the person is expressing, tiny machines under the robot's silicone skin remould its face to mimic what it sees. For Hara, heads are just the beginning. His goal is to design a humanoid robot that is interactive, friendly, and most of all, familiar. But do we really want a robot that looks just like us? Maybe not.

Fumio Hara poses with a skeleton of one of his face robots (above). The face robot's network of wires and pulleys are covered in a flexible skin (below).

In the late 1970s, Japanese robot engineer Masahiro Mori did some fascinating research on how human beings interact with robots. Mori discovered that people like friendly-looking mechanical robots. But Mori found that when robots look too human-like, people stop liking them. Mori called this sudden shift the Uncanny Valley, the place where people begin to feel uncomfortable with human-like robots.

Mind and Matter

As scientists try to 'teach' robots emotional understanding, they are also trying to program robots to think for themselves. It's called AI, artificial intelligence, and it's a tall order indeed. AI is the attempt to get a computer to work like the human brain. If we can do that, we will be able to build the ultimate robot – an artificial version of ourselves.

In 1950, British scientist Alan Turing said that there were two ways to go about creating artificial intelligence. In the top-down approach, human beings teach the computer everything they know. The other method, called bottom-up, mimics the way we learn – a little at a time, building upon previous knowledge and experiences. You might imagine top-down as swallowing an entire library and bottom-up as snacking on one book at a time, starting with books for young readers.

As early as 1944, Alan Turing spoke of his plans to 'build a brain'.

In the 1950s, most scientists, including Turing, preferred the top-down approach. Just write a program that tells a computer what to do, step-by-step. If you put that computer into a robot, there would never be any surprises because the programmer would always know what the robot's computer brain knew.

In 1966, scientists at the Stanford Research Institute (renamed SRI Technology in 1970) in California, USA, began building Shakey. This was the first intelligent, autonomous (operating competely on its own) robot. Shakey was actually able to plan the steps needed to perform simple tasks, such as moving wooden blocks around. The problem was, Shakey took forever to do anything. Its computer was so slow that it spent most of its time thinking.

Since then, computers have become very speedy indeed, but they are still incredibly slow compared to the processing power of the human brain. Also, computers don't work like a human brain. Humans learn from experience and store that information for the future. They can also quickly adapt their thinking to different situations. So if we want our robots to think the way we do, we're going to have to build a computer that can learn the way we do. This, believe it or not, is slowly but surely happening.

Experience is the Best Teacher

Engineers have begun building robots that can adapt to their environment. They operate on what are called patterns of behaviour.

Most of these robots are quite small and behave a lot like insects. Insects don't really think. They rely on their senses and instincts to find food and to survive in an ever-changing world. Like insects, the little

A robotic ladybird, developed by Sanyo Electric Company, sits on a leaf.

insect-bots have been equipped for sensing their physical environment. But they have not been preprogrammed with any data about their environment. So when they are first turned on, they're brainless.

But the insect-bots' computers are programmed with separate 'layers of behaviour'. The behaviour layers help an insect-bot learn about its environment. The more it learns, the more it can do. Once the insect-bot has mastered one layer of behaviour, the next higher layer of behaviour kicks in. With each layer, the insect-bot gets better at dealing with the world around it.

Flying Robots

Since 1998, engineers at the University of California, Berkeley, USA, have been working on a micromechanical flying insect (MFI) project. To design their MFIs, the engineers study how real flying insects take-off, use their wings and bodies and move through the air. The engineers continue to work on making the MFIs autonomous, lightweight and flexible.

At MIT, James McLurkin has built robot ants using these layers of behavior. But McLurkin's ant-bots are even more amazing because they are able to signal to each other when they find ant-bot 'food'. In other words, the ant-bots learn how to cooperate to achieve a shared goal. The ultimate ant-bot, however, is yet to come – one that can communicate with real ants.

'I believe', said Hans Moravec, a research professor at Carnegie Mellon, 'that robots with human intelligence will be common within the next 50 years.' Certainly, the Center for Intelligent Systems (CIS) at Vanderbilt University in Tennessee, USA, shows how close we are getting. The CIS has developed a robot called ISAC (for Intelligent Soft Arm Control). ISAC can express emotion and has both short-term and long-term memory. And because this robot's brain has been designed to 'think' much like ours, ISAC may actually be able to dream.

ISAC (above) was built to help people who have physical disabilities. Improvements focus on learning skills and response to human emotions.

It seems almost certain that in the future we will be sharing our planet with a strange new form of robotic life. What we build in the lab will have the potential to become as smart as we are. It may even improve upon its own technology. Will we love these robots or fear them? Time will tell.

Glossary

android: a mobile robot built in human form

artificial intelligence: the study of how computers can be designed to work and learn like a human brain, for use in robotics

computer: an electronic machine designed to store and process information using a mathematical system

humanoid: having human characteristics, such as facial features

Internet: an information system of interconnected computers. On the Internet, a computer user can communicate with other Internet users and access information from millions of resources.

manipulators: the type of robot most commonly used in factories. Manipulators are usually simple robots that perform one type of job, such as welding cars or packing boxes.

medical robots: robots designed to help doctors in diagnosing and treating patients

patterns of behaviour: an approach to artificial intelligence in which computers are programmed to learn information by experience

robotics: the science of designing and creating robots

robots: machines that can perform tasks and jobs through computer programming and movable parts

service robots: robots designed to interact with humans and perform helpful tasks in homes or businesses

survival instinct: a function programmed into some computers that allows them to act to avoid damage or destruction

Uncanny Valley: the point at which humans become uncomfortable with the life-like qualities of a humanoid robot

Source Notes

For quoted material:

p. 40 (caption), The Alan Turing Home Page, http://www.turing.org.uk/turing (October 2004).

p. 43, Hans Moravec, *Mind Children,* Cambridge, MA: Harvard University Press, 1988.

Selected Bibliography

Aylett, Ruth. *Robots: Bringing Intelligent Machines to Life.* Hauppauge, NY: Barron's Educational Series, 2002.

Bruce, Allison, Illah Nourbakhsh, and Reid Simmons. *The Role of Expressiveness and Attention in Human-Robot Interaction.* Proceedings of the IEEE International Conference on Robotics and Automation (ICRA 02), May 2002.

Kirsner, Scott. *They're Robots? Those Beasts! New York Times,* 16 September 2004, E1.

Mars Exploration Rover Mission, Jet Propulsion Laboratory of the National Aeronautics and Space Agency, http://marsrovers.jpl.nasa.gov (October 2004).

Moravec, Hans. *Mind Children.* Cambridge, MA: Harvard University Press, 1988.

Paul, Gregory S, and Earl D Cox. *Beyond Humanity: CyberEvolution and Future Minds.* Rockland, MA: Charles River Media, Inc, 1996.

Quinlan, Heather. *Oh, the Humanity*! The Learning Channel Online, http://tlc.discovery.com/convergence/robosapiens/article.html (May 2004).

Telotte, J P. *Replications: A Robotic History of the Science Fiction Film.* Chicago: University of Illinois Press, 1995.

Whitehouse, David. *'Tiny Robots Flex Their Plastic Muscles',* British Broadcasting Corporation (BBC) News Online, http://news.bbc.co.uk/1/hi/sci/tech/811314.stm (June 29, 2000).

Further Reading and Websites

Bridgman, Roger. *Robot* (Eyewitness Guide) Dorling Kindersley Publishers Ltd, 2004.

Gifford, Clive. *Robots* (Technology All Around US) Franklin Watts Ltd, 2005.

Graham, Ian. *Military Technology* (New Technology) Evans Brothers, 2008

Rooney, Anne. *Computers* (Technology All Around US) Franklin Watts Ltd, 2005.

Snedden, Robert. *Medical Technology* (New Technology) Evans Brothers, 2008.

Tyndall, Elizabeth. *Robots* Longman, 2004.

Kismet

> http://www.ai.mit.edu/projects/humanoid-robotics-group/kismet/kismet.html
> The Humanoid Robotics Lab at MIT runs a website dedicated to Kismet, the 'sociable robot'. The site includes photos and videos, information about the project and short biographies of the people involved in Kismet's design.

Mars Exploration Rover Mission

> http://marsrovers.jpl.nasa.gov/home/index.html
> NASA's Jet Propulsion Laboratory website features the latest news on Spirit and Opportunity. Photos from the surface of Mars, information about the planet and details of the Rover project are included.

Robots

> http://www.robot.org.uk/
> This site has loads of information on building robots, contests, robotic events and robotic kits.

Robotics

> http://www.thetech.org/robotics/
> The Tech Museum of Innovation's Robotics website features a robotics timeline, a history of many types of robots and an essay on the ethical issues behind robotic technology.

Index

Adkins, Doug 23
Aibo 32, 33
Alaska Volcano
   Observatory 15
American Open. *See*
   International RoboCup
   Federation
android 7
ant-bot 43
Ariel 26–27
artificial intelligence 40;
   bottom-up approach,
   40; top-down approach,
   40. *See also* patterns of
   behaviour
Artificial Intelligence
   Laboratory. *See*
   Massachusetts Institute
   of Technology (MIT)
ASIMO 29–30, 33
automata 6
automation 7, 8, 9
autonomy 20, 41

biomimetics 29
Breazeal, Cynthia 36
Bruce, Allison 35

California Institute of
   Technology 22
Capek, Karel 10
Carnegie Mellon
   University 12, 14, 15, 32,
   43; Robotics Institute 35
Case Western Reserve
   University (CWRU) 26
Center for Intelligent
   Systems (CIS) 43
cockroach robot 26

da Vinci, Leonardo
   6–7
Dante II 16–17

DARPA Challenge 13
Deep Space Network
   (DSN) 19
Defense Advanced
   Research Projects
   Agency (DARPA) 13
degrees of independence
   20. *See also* autonomy
Department of Defense
   (DOD) 13
Dr Who 4

ENIAC 9
exploratory robots 15–22
explosive ordnance
   disposal (EOD) robots
   14–15

face robots 38–39
Feelix 36

Gantenbrink, Rudolf 21, 22
Great Pyramid of Giza
   20–22

Hanson, David 38, 39
Hara, Fumio 39

hazardous waste robots
   14, 15
Hollywood 4–5, 23
homunculi 6, 7
Honda Motor Co Ltd,
   29
humanoid 7, 39

I, Robot 4, 5
industrial robots 10–13
insect-bot 41–42
Institute and Museum of
   the History of Science 7
International RoboCup
   Federation 32;
   American Open 32–33

Internet 16, 30
ISAC 43

Japan 25, 31, 39
Jaquet-Droz, Pierre 8

K-bot 38
Kismet 36–37
Kobayashi, Hiroshi 39

Leg Laboratory. *See*
   Massachusetts Institute
   of Technology
Legos, 36

manipulators 11–12, 13
Mars Exploration Rovers
   18–20
Massachusetts Institute of
   Technology (MIT) 42;
   Artificial Intelligence
   Laboratory 36; Leg
   Laboratory 28–29
Matsuoka, Yoky 12
mechanization 7, 8, 9
medical robots 22–23, 25
micro-bots 23
miocromechanical flying
   insects (MFIs) 42
miniaturization 8, 9–10
Monopod 28
Moravec, Hans 43
Mori, Masahiro 39

National Aeronautics and
   Space Administration
   (NASA) 15, 18, 19

Opportunity. *See also*
   Mars Exploration Rovers

patterns of behaviour
   41–43
programmability 7, 8, 9,

10, 27, 28, 40–41
pyramid. *See* Great
Pyramid of Giza
QRIO, 31

robot: definition of 7, 10;
types of 5, 7, 10–11, 13,
14–15, 20, 22–23, 24–25
robotics 5, 13, 38, 39, 43;
anatomy 12, 13, 16, 25,
27; beginnings of 6–8;
and computer science
8–10, 30; emotional
responsiveness 31, 33,
34–39, 43; mobility and
movement 13, 16, 24,

25, 26–33. *See also*
artificial intelligence
Robotics Institute. *See*
Carnegie Mellon
University
robotic vehicles 13
*RUR (Rossum's Universal
Robots)* 10

Sandia National
Laboratory 22, 23
Scribe, the 8
service robots 24–25
snake-bot 22
Sony Corporation 31
Spirit. See Mars

Exploration Rovers
SRI Technology 41
Star Wars 4
survival instinct 20

Toyota 31
Troody 28, 29
trumpet-playing robot 31
Turing, Alan 40

Uncanny Valley 40
University of California,
Berkeley 25
Upuaut-2 21–22

Vanderbilt University 43

Photo Acknowledgements

Photographs are used with the permission of: © Todd Strand/Independent Picture Service, p1, all backgrounds; © Forest J. Ackerman Collection/CORBIS, p 4; © John Springer Collection/CORBIS, p 5 (top); © Columbia Pictures/Photofest, p 5 (bottom); © Bettmann/CORBIS, p 7; Musée d'art et d'histoire, Neuchâtel (Suisse), p 8; University of Pennsylvania's School of Engineering and Applied Science, p 9; © Charles O'Rear/CORBIS, pp 10, 11; The Robotics Institute, Carnegie Mellon University, p 12; © David McNew/Getty Images, p 13; © Peter Russell; The Military Picture Library/CORBIS, p 15; NASA, p 16; © ANDY CLARK/Reuters/CORBIS, p 17; © Reuters/CORBIS, pp 18 (top) 19, 25; © NASA/JPL/Handout/Reuters/CORBIS, p 18 (centre); © AFP/Getty Images, p 18 (bottom) ; © Royalty-Free/CORBIS, p 20; AP Photo/Mohammad al Sehety, p 21; © Randy Montoya/Sandia National Laboratories/Newsmakers/Getty Images, p 22 (top); Toshifumi Kitamura/AFP/Getty Images, p 22 (bottom); © Getty Images, p 23; courtesy of Daniel Kingsley, Roger Quinn and Roy Ritzmann, Case Western Reserve University, p 26 (top and centre); © Tom Young/CORBIS, p 26 (bottom); Donna Coveney/Massachusetts Institute of Technology, p 28; courtesy of American Honda Motor Co, Inc, ASIMO division, p 30; © Ramin Talaie/CORBIS, p 31 (top); © Haruyoshi Yamaguchi/CORBIS, p 31 (bottom); courtesy of Tucker Balch, GVU Center, Georgia Institute of Technology, p 32; courtesy of Sony Electronics, Inc, p 33; courtesy of Alison Bruce, The Robotics Institute, Carnegie Mellon University, p 35; © Jakob Fredslund, p 36; © Rick Friedman/CORBIS, p 37; © David Hanson, p 38 (top left and bottom right); AP Photo/Tony Gutierrez, p 38 (top centre and right), (bottom left and centre); © Peter Menzel, p 39 (both); courtesy of Lady Nicola Turing, p 40; © MASTER PHOTO SYNDICATION/CORBIS SYGMA, p 42; courtesy of Flo Fottrell and Kazuhiko Kawamura, Center For Intelligent Systems, Vanderbilt University, p 43.

Cover: AP Photo/Tony Gutierrez (main); Courtesy of American Honda Motor Co, Inc, ASIMO division (top); NASA (centre); courtesy of Flo Fottrell and Kazuhiko Kawamura, Center for Intelligent Systems, Vanderbilt University (bottom); © Todd Strand/Independent Picture Service (background). Back cover: © Todd Strand/ Independent Picture Service (background)